Silence as Yoga

BY
SWAMI PARAMANANDA

VEDANTA CENTRE PUBLISHERS
COHASSET

FOURTH EDITION
Copyright © 1974 by
Vedanta Centre, Inc.
All rights reserved.

published by
Vedanta Centre
130 Beechwood Street
Cohasset, Mass. 02025

ISSBN 0-911564-11

Printed in U.S.A.

CONTENTS

PREFACE

In ancient India the yogi who sought to realize his divine Self would retreat to the seclusion of the forest or to the quiet of a Himalayan cave. There, plunged into meditation and other spiritual disciplines, he would hear the whisper of his inner voice and establish communion with that One who dwells within.

The spiritual aspirant of today sits down to meditate to the accompaniment of zooming jets overhead and blaring radios from next door. Where can he find the silence which will reveal the truth of his depths? Swami Paramananda, in the series of lectures which follows, answers: He can find that silence within himself and enter into it so completely that he will not be disturbed or distracted by any external commotion. True silence is a state of consciousness which man attains through the control of his own mind, heart, and speech.

Having attained this, he carries it with him, emanating an atmosphere of silent blessing which surrounds him even in midtown Manhattan or downtown Los Angeles.

As the blight of "noise pollution" increasingly harasses our outer world, let us counteract it on the deepest level, by discovering that impenetrable stillness in our own being and radiating that peace to our fellow-men, with the wordless power that touches all souls.

Gayatri Devi

Cohasset
September, 1974

SILENCE

HUSH! This is the hour of silence
When soul seeks its refreshment.

Turbulent mind, thou art ever restive for
sport and gain;

Thou art ever mad for new sensation and
art in feverish plight.

Wouldst thou rob me of my true happiness?

Be still, that thou mayest not miss this
new and blessed joy.

How sweet is the sound of silence!

How tender is its touch!

How fragrant is its breathing!

How lovely is its form!

O be still yet awhile that my soul may see
and feel, hear and touch its own in
this realm of peace divine.

I.

THE CREATIVE POWER OF SILENCE

I am the Silence of secrets; I am the Wisdom of the wise.—*Bhagavad-Gita.*

When thou prayest enter into thy closet, and when thou hast shut thy door, pray to thy Father which is in secret; and thy Father, which seeth in secret shall reward thee openly.—*Jesus the Christ.*

His thought is quiet, quiet are his word and deed, when he has obtained freedom by true knowledge, when he has thus become a quiet man.—*Buddha.*

A SEED in the womb of mother earth lies in silence absorbing nourishment and other natural blessings until its expanded soul bursts forth into blossom. The spirit of genius, nurtured in the bosom of quiet contemplation, awaits patiently its appointed hour of awakening. Silence, the great unseen power, the miracle of life, works upon our character with strange contrast. At times it overwhelms us with its oppressive stillness, and again it falls upon our heart as a shower of refreshing raindrops on a sultry summer day. How often silence acts as a tonic, invigorating and reviving our dull spirit. Then at other times its effect upon us is like that of a narcotic, putting our life's energies into a state of morbid sleep. All great forces of nature work in contrast.

In the world of religion and philosophy the practice of silence plays a most vital part. It creates an atmosphere and enables the seeker to find access to an inner sanctuary entirely hidden from the restless and turbulent material world. Whenever we are listening to fine music if some one speaks or makes a noise we are distracted, and jarred by it, and often we lose the subtle beauty of the music. Similarly in spiritual study if our attention is diverted we receive little or no benefit. That is the reason why the idea of complete silence before spiritual study is strongly advocated by many of the great schools of thought. We can easily see its technical reason, how it aids us in the act of concentration, but its more profound significance is in the unfoldment of our higher nature. Even today, we find that many places of worship maintain rigid silence in order to create an atmosphere so needful for spiritual devotion and prayer. We can never hear the language of the soul if our ears are filled with the loud noises of the world. One of the Sufi mystics expresses the import of this beautifully. "Be silent that the Lord Who gave thee language may speak, for as He fashioned a door and lock, He has also made a key. . . . I am silent. Speak Thou, O Soul of Soul of Soul."

All the mystic teachers and illumined sages emanate a peculiar atmosphere of calm and quiet dignity. In India some of the great seers completely refrain from speech and yet they exert a most potent influence upon the lives of their followers. One of the first forms of spiritual discipline the neophytes have to undergo is the practice of silence. They never speak before their teachers unless they are asked to do so. What is the most direct blessing they receive through it? It makes their mind receptive and whatever it receives it can easily assimilate. The necessity of this is felt even in our secular education. Unless the mind is receptive any amount of time expended in study is of very little avail. It is interesting to note how Madame Montessori in her system of education advocates this idea of silence. Its value was felt in India from time immemorial and was widely practised from child-education to the advanced Vedic revelation. This mode of living and thinking, however, is quite out of fashion with our modern life and habit. There are some who even feel a strong aversion to it and this is because they confuse the idea of silence with dullness and inaction.

The aim of silence is not to free our mind from thought and assume a state of emptiness and passivity. On the contrary silence becomes a definite factor for our efficient and concentrated thought. Silence means co-ordination of our body, our mind, and all our faculties to such an extent that every particle moves in one rhythm. In this state all our aspirations and ideals work in harmony, so much so that there is no friction. You can verify this in connection with machinery; that which avoids friction most makes the least noise and endures the longest. In the world of life and all forms of activity, we find this to be true. The life that moves without inharmony and friction is the most efficient life. A man whose mind is well-ordered and whose whole system is well-organized is always finding something of interest within himself. He does not offer his opinion to others because he has found something within. He has become quiet, and through his balance of mind and attitude he is always discovering an inner interest. That is what the Indo-Aryans recognized as the most essential factor in all forms of study. No one can study successfully unless he has the power of concentration and co-ordination, and this power cannot be achieved unless we come to an attitude of silence. A silent being is a very restful being. Even in a household we find that a person who is calm, composed and thoughtful radiates a powerful influence. Nervously disorganized people find a great source of rest through him.

One of the most interesting phenomena that takes place in connection with the practice of silence is that the mind evolves creative genius. For instance when a person who is used to intense activity and outer diversion for his pastime and pleasure is thrown suddenly on his own inner resources, if he is not thwarted by it, his mind will have a peculiar reaction and he will discover his inherent reserve and originality. This also is true in connection with children's education. If we do not try to keep their minds altogether occupied with artificial toys and noisy games, they will work and invent newer ones, and this quickening of the inner faculties is the gist of true education. We think better when our mind is not weighted down by matter. We see more clearly when our eyes are focussed on a single objective and nothing is more efficacious towards this end than the practice of silence.

All wise people realize that the deeper part of our nature can only be expressed effectively when our outer being is still. That is why so often they retire from the crowd. They are not keen to offer their opinions. They think deeply and act quietly. We frequently misunderstand people of this type who are not constantly active like ourselves. We imagine that their lives are wasteful because they are not forever engaged in outer occupation; but we can never measure the good that radiates from a calm and contemplative spirit. Phillips Brooks expresses this beautifully: "Certainly, in our own little sphere, it is not the most active people to whom we owe the most. Among the common people whom we know, it is not necessarily those who are busiest, not those who, meteor-like, are ever on the rush after some visible charge and work. It is the lives, like the stars, which simply pour down on us the calm light of their bright and faithful being, up to which we look and out of which we gather the deepest calm and courage. It seems to me that there is reassurance here for many of us who seem to have no chance for active usefulness. We can do nothing for our fellow-men. But still it is good to know that we can be something for them; to know (and this we may know surely) that no man or woman of the humblest sort can really be strong, gentle, pure and good, without the world being better for it, without somebody being helped and comforted by the very existence of that goodness."

We must have certain fundamental virtues before we can make any headway with our spiritual life. If our mind is filled with noble thoughts we do not find ourselves lonely and unprotected at any time. The average person is lonely whenever there is no one to entertain him or talk with him, but a person who has entered into his spiritual depth, even in a small measure, is very glad to find an opportunity when he can be alone, communing with his inner Self. We should all learn to be alone with ourselves. People imagine that they cannot be happy unless they are constantly in the company of others. Then again some think that they must get away from everything and everybody in order to have peace of mind. However, we are never alone even though we may enter a mountain cave if we are tormented by our own ignorance and selfishness. You may wonder what I mean by silence if it is not getting away from the crowd, if it is not breaking away from the noisy part of life. It does not mean that. It requires something more than running away from people. You may enter the forest's untravelled depths and yet you may find no quiet if your own mind is noisy, if your own attitude is distracted **or** if you have not harmony within your own self. These are the things which we have to cultivate and it is better for us to cultivate them before we fall into the entanglement of life.

We cannot go into this world and expect to find everything just the way we should like it. There are disappointments and unexpected happenings, but in spite of all these upheavals we can carry ourselves safely and with poise if we have acquired the silent attitude of mind and habit. You may believe intellectually that it is a wrong thing to be angry, it is a wrong thing to be impatient, it is a wrong thing to speak harshly; but the words come unexpectedly, and before you realize it you have spoken unkindly. We can order our mind in such rhythm and connect our life with higher forces to such an extent that these calamities will never befall us.

The great secret of success is that we work with our whole being, and we cannot do this without being absolutely still and concentrated. These are the simple facts of life, but not so easy to accomplish. We cannot expect somebody else to do it for us. There are many people who would like to have others think for them. Even the greatest mind cannot think for another. We are never going to gain our heart's satisfaction, or our highest wisdom, in that way. Another mind and another brain cannot think out our problem, because it does not know the entire situation. We cannot give a true picture to any one no matter how we may try. There is, however, a way of finding our own solution, and that is by learning to enter within our own depth.

It is not work so much that wears us out; sometimes lack of work may do it. It is not knowing how to direct ourselves;

it is not knowing how to find that attitude of collectedness and poise. When we are equipped with these qualities we always have greater power of penetration. Intellectually we may grasp the value of all this, but that is only the ethical aspect of it. It is the most dynamic, most practical and most valuable thing in life when we apply it, and only when we apply it in our life do we find its fruition. A person who is nervous ceases to be nervous; a person who is physically weak and disorganized, gradually becomes calm, and a person who is dull, without any power of magnetism or attraction, suddenly blossoms and has a certain amount of light. Now this comes from within, and for that reason it has a far-reaching effect. There are many people who can talk and preach and make a noise, but nothing superficial can bring us satisfaction. It is by living quietly and earnestly that we evolve the true spiritual insight which enables us to find our intrinsic value.

Great ideas and ideals are always before us. Everybody hears them, but when a genuine soul hears an idea he takes it; he says, I must know more about it. He thinks, reflects and meditates. He goes into his very inmost depth, and then he brings it to fruition. However, this does not come to a man who is in haste and wants everything at once. That is one of our greatest calamities. The things we acquire by long, steadfast, devoted effort are the things which last and bring into our life great richness. Therefore we must abandon as soon as we can this idea of haste and immediate results. The deep things do not come suddenly. Let us be patient,—patient with ourselves. We may recognize many defects in our nature; but no matter how much blemish we may have within, or how much disorder, it can all be removed. Go on working silently. If you do not succeed at once, put more energy and force into it. One who is willing to wait, the very attitude saves him and enables him to surmount insurmountable difficulties, while one who is impatient, he loses his opportunities. Therefore silence and patience go together. Silence has a wonderful creative power. Make a study of the lives of great men. They conceive an idea but they do not go out and shout it before the world, they think silently and work quietly until they realize their ideal.

If we can form the habit of devoting a certain time to silent relaxation, it will have a very definite beneficial effect upon both our physical and moral being. When in course of our daily round of duties we find ourselves growing physically tired or mentally tense, if we can

take an attitude of relaxation and co-
ordinate our thoughts, discarding all
feelings of vexation and unrest, we shall
feel restored and refreshed. It will even
enable us to do our work better. How
often people go to bed after their day's
labor and do not rest. The next morning
they wake up feeling very weary, without any sense of freshness or repose.
What is the cause of it? They were not
working at night. No, but they were
worrying about their work. They took
their work, all their worries and anxie-
ties, to bed with them. That is not the
way to order our life. There is time for
work; there is time for recreation and
rest, and silence is the best rest-giver.
There is nothing which can rest us more
quickly than the attitude of silence, and
every one has the right to it. When all
is still, when our thoughts are quieted
down and our entire nervous system is

in order, when we have naught against
any one and our mind is calm and
poised, then in the inner depth of stillness we find something which is so en-
nobling and restful that others even feel
it.

> How sweet is the sound of silence!
> How tender is its touch!
> How fragrant is its breathing!
> How lovely is its form!
> O be still yet awhile that my soul may see and
> feel, hear and touch its own in this realm of
> peace divine.

There are delicate things in our life,
most potent and most vibrant, but we
fail to perceive them because we lack in
delicacy of feeling. When we are distracted by visible material glamour we
miss our mark, but in that hour of silent
co-ordination, when all our faculties are
in perfect tune, we realize that we are
part of the cosmic Being. It is in this
hour we find the fullness of our life, for
then our little life has become united

with the great Life, and our little mind
with the cosmic Mind. Only at such
moments when the finite and Infinite
are so commingled does our mind stand
apart in speechless silence and unspoken
wonder.

II.

SILENCE AND CO-ORDINATION

Observing the vow of silence, when one begins to set his mind on Yoga (spiritual practices), then discrimination and knowledge and power to avoid evil are gained by him.—*Mahabharata.*

Beware of the fool whose volume of words is as that of ten men—a hundred arrows shot and each one wide of the target. If thou art wise, shoot one, and that one straight.—*Bustan of Sadi.*

If water derives lucidity from stillness, how much more the faculties of the mind! The mind of the sage, being in repose, becomes the mirror of the universe, the speculum of all creation.—*Chuang Tzu.*

WHAT sleep does for our body and nervous system, silence does for our mind and spirit. All the discordant conditions in our life are greatly due to our lack of co-ordination of both physical and mental forces. Until we learn to think and act with calm and unruffled attitude, we cannot make our life productive. The practice of silence is a very great help for acquiring evenness of mind and tranquility of body. The silence which leads to efficiency, however, is not a negation, a state merely of sitting and doing nothing. It is experienced only when the whole being has been unified and is flowing through one channel in perfect rhythm.

The productiveness of our activity depends entirely on what we put into it and in order to put our best into each thought and action, we need to order our mind, to gather up all its scattered forces, to establish our equilibrium; and we cannot do this unless we withdraw at intervals from the haste and noise of outer occupations. That is why Yogis and those who are seeking earnestly for light look upon the practice of silence as essential to their spiritual progress. In the first place it enables us to store up a great deal of life force which now we expend unwisely in needless talking. We wear ourselves out, disturb others, and say much which might better be left unsaid when we talk constantly. We· also dull the mind and lessen its power of penetration. All spiritual vision and deeper understanding are unfolded in the hours of silent reflection. It is in the moment of silence that we hear the voice of the Infinite. When our ears are listening to the loud voices of the world, we cannot know that another voice is speaking in our heart. Therefore, those who have obtained direct vision of Truth are not inclined to make their own voice heard.

The productive life is always a silent life. When a man is creating something, he is not inclined to talk. He becomes rapt in thought and gradually through his concentrated thought he gains access to the hidden recesses of nature. He does not squander his forces by telling each little revelation as it comes to him. Sri Ramakrishna gives us the parable of the pearl oyster. It comes to the surface of the water to catch a raindrop falling at the auspicious moment when the star

Svati is in ascendancy. Then it goes down to the bottom of the sea and remains there until the pearl is formed. The same is true of the genuine seeker after wisdom. As soon as he has found his access to God, he becomes deep and silent.

Silence is considered so necessary in India that there are great sages who become *Munis*, or silent ones. Some of them take the vow of complete silence and direct all their physical and mental forces toward spiritual illumination. Others refrain from speaking of non-essential matters. Through the observance of the vow of silence they become gifted in prophecy and power to bless others. Even the atmosphere of the place where they live is charged with a definite spiritual force. An example is given in one of our sacred books of a youthful sage, radiant with illumination, sitting in meditation under a banyan tree. A disciple, old and weary with life's cares, approached him with mind and heart full of doubt and depression. The disciple asked many questions, but even though the teacher ever remained silent the doubts of the disciple were destroyed and he went away in peace. This shows us that if the Light of Truth shines within us clearly without obstruction it will reach and enlighten others. It is not in India alone that they hold this view that a person does not have to talk in order to impart his teaching; it is shared by many of the mystics and seers of the world. A parallel instance is given by Plato. "I will tell you, Socrates," says Aristides, "a thing incredible but nevertheless true, I made a great proficiency when I associated with you, even if I was only in the same house, though not in the same room; but more so when I was in the same room; and much more when I looked at you. But I made by far the greatest proficiency when I sat near you and touched you."

Yet you may say, what can a silent man do? His scope of usefulness must be very limited. The greatest amount of good in the world is not done by the talker or even by the worker who is constantly busy with his hands and feet, but by the one who has found the true centre of his being. His very existence throws radiance into the lives of countless people. We may have a great desire to help others, but if we have not found the remedy for evil in our own life, even our best intentions will not do much for them. These *Munis* may not speak, but they have the burning effulgence of the spiritual light within themselves. Their life itself is an expression of Truth, and whether they speak or not, they are constantly shedding their holy influence on others.

If we would help ourselves and our fellow-beings, therefore, we must take certain hours when we can shut out the noise of the world and commune with the Infinite. The deeper themes of life we can discover only when our mind is not disturbed by worldly agitations. Even a scientist, a musician, an artist must have communion with his ideal, and this cannot be done without silence.

The practice of silence, however, does not mean merely refraining from speech. It means stilling the vital energies so that there is a cessation of all activity both inner and outer. The body must be without motion, the mind must be serene and heart tranquil. We cannot accomplish this by merely withdrawing to a secluded spot. It is an interior quality rather. Outer conditions may aid us tremendously in attaining it, but without the inner poise it is impossible to reach.

Our thoughts grow undisturbed and uninterrupted on the silent soil of the mind. In silence we are able to think better and we are able to express our ideas through our outer actions more effectively. When we cultivate this we gain not only greater efficiency, but also fortify ourselves with the wonderful blessing of a serene attitude. People who are used to talking much, it is better for them to talk less and less, and learn to act with more quiet and composed bearing. Almost invariably we find that those who talk in excess are those who think less clearly and collectedly. An idle tongue is one of the greatest curses. It not only hurts the person who is directly responsible for it, but disturbs the peace of mind of many others. Sri

Chaitanya, one of India's foremost saints, taught his disciples never to take part in gossip. He said that they should not only refrain from making gossip, but should never even listen to any idle talk, for by doing so they only encouraged the mischief-mongers. We cannot possibly conceive any lofty thought or lift our prayer to the Divine until our mind and heart are full of serenity.

The practice of physical silence restores our body and sense organs. The practice of mental silence refreshes our mind and quickens all our inner faculties. The power gained through it is tremendous. When we undertake anything hastily and nervously, we make mistakes and have to do it over, thus wasting our time and energies. Without deliberation and balance we can accomplish nothing worth while, and a moment of silence before each task enables us to maintain our balance. Its physical benefit is apparent at once. If we learn to bring ourselves to a state of absolute stillness, checking all unnecessary expenditure of force, our whole body is refreshed and strengthened. This reacts on the mind and makes it alert and free. Even from the point of view of worldly advantage, therefore, it is wise to practise silence. The majority of people have a very false standard of life. They imagine that when two or three human beings are together, they must always entertain each other. Often nature is providing us with inspiration and we miss it, because of this foolish habit. Why should we suppose that whenever we are with others we must always talk? It means that our mind is empty. The noble mind is one that is filled from within and does not need continual diversion from without. It is not dependent or demanding. Its thought is calm and deep and still. Only as we become more and more silent will our inward life unfold.

When we have conceived an idea, if we put it into words, the greater part of its strength is dissipated and its success is rendered doubtful. Is not the logic of this evident? As soon as we draw our mind away from the idea itself and begin to discuss it, we set up counter currents of thought, our mental strength is expended in combating these and little is left to carry our idea to fulfillment. If we would be successful we must conceive in the silence, work in the silence and achieve in the silence. Great things are always done silently. Whenever a life is fruitful, we shall always find that it is a silent life. If we would make our endeavor more productive, we must try never to talk unnecessarily. It is a wonderful thing to have a controlled tongue. When we have established balance at this

point, we shall find that the other parts
of our being will become balanced and
our whole life will gain new rhythm and
illumination. In India they adopt the
simple practice that before they eat, or
drink, or study, or go to sleep, or undertake any business, they sit in silence for
a moment and try to unite themselves
with the centre of their being. When we
are distracted by outer conditions or con-
cerns, we lose our sense of proportion and
we cannot do well what we have to do.
As long as our physical eyes lead us to see
the many, we cannot see the one; so the
devotee closes his outer eyes that he may
open his inner eye and with it perceive the
deeper realities within. He closes his
outer ears that he may hear the voice of
the Infinite in his heart.

The practice of silence has a profound
significance when we embrace the spiritual life. As only still waters reflect the

perfect image, so only on the surface of the silent heart do we receive the unbroken image of Truth. Knowledge always destroys our ignorance and unrest, and we cannot increase our knowledge until we go down into the quiet recesses of our inner being. We must give ourselves a chance. There is not one who is not hungering for perfect health, for perfect peace and happiness; but these cannot come to us unless we create the right conditions for them. If we learn to live right, to think right, to make our life balanced and tranquil, we shall reap the result in a fuller expression of spiritual perfection. Now our ears do not hear the voice of the Supreme. The great teachers tell us to listen to that voice, to be guided by that voice. The ordinary man says that he cannot hear it; that it is all an imagination; but the mystic hears it, because he has made his outer being silent and has found access to the inner shrine of his soul.

When we begin to live the spiritual life, we touch a deeper note and we cease to judge from the surface. All differences are to be found only on the surface and one who lives constantly on the surface does not see the connecting link between man and man, between one soul and another; but he who has learned to live below the surface sees unity everywhere. He is not dependent on human judgments; he is not influenced by the world. He is wholly guided and protected by the Divine. In all his undertakings he is led by the hand of God. To him God is more real than any creature of flesh and blood. He walks with God; he talks with God; he lives with God. His whole being is centered in God, so that, whether he speaks or does not speak, he expresses the thought of God. He does not have to use

words to do it. Rather he knows that the
Infinite can never find full expression in
finite words. Therefore in the Vedas it is
said that the glory of the Supreme is beyond mind and speech.

It is the ignorant man who claims
loudly that his belief is the only belief,
his path the only path; but one whose vision has become expanded through a
larger realization grows dumb and his
silence is the most eloquent expression of
Truth. Let our lips sometimes be dumb
that our heart may sing the glory of the
Infinite. Let us give our inner being a
chance to listen to the voice which is too
subtle for the physical ear to hear. If for
a few moments only each day we can still
the noisy energies of our mind and body
and learn to practise true silence, it will
create a dynamo of spiritual power and
elevate our whole being to the lofty
heights of a new consciousness.

III.

THE SERVICE OF SILENT LIVING

Keep thine own sentiments and faith to thyself. Do not talk about them abroad, otherwise thou wilt be a great loser. Keep thyself aloof at the time of thy devotions from those who scoff at them and those who ridicule piety and the pious.—*Sri Ramakrishna.*

Let thy speech be better than silence, or be silent.
—Dionysius the Elder.

Silence is a healing for all ailments. Silence is good for the wise; how much more so for the foolish. All my days I have grown up amongst the wise, and I have found naught of better service than silence.—*Ancient Jewish Proverb.*

THE definite sign of a spiritually-minded person is his silent, tolerant attitude. Bees, until they have found the flower and tasted the honey, make a loud, buzzing noise; but the moment they taste the honey, they become absorbed and cease to make any sound. So it is with us. Before we find the Truth, we argue and dispute and challenge others who differ from us; but when we come in contact with something deeper, we grow silent and do not try to force it on other minds. We try to live it in our own life; and as we live it in our own life, inevitably it reaches other lives.

Spiritual qualities are infectious just as evil qualities are. One bad person can drag down many others by his evil propensities; while those who have noble ideals and loving characters uplift others merely by their silent influence. When we study external conditions, it is sometimes very discouraging to see how slowly this influence works; but it can never fail absolutely. And if we wish to produce a lasting effect on any character, it is better not to have it work too quickly. When we set fire to hay, it makes a tremendous blaze, then in a moment it is all over; while a log fire, which takes a long time to kindle, burns steadily and is dependable. Similarly in spiritual awakening, if the person is over-enthusiastic and emotionally excited, he exhausts his forces and the effect wears off. If, on the contrary, his deeper nature is touched, it may not show much outwardly, but the result endures.

The best help we can bring to others is not by word of mouth or by any active exertion; the really vital help, that which is lasting and far-reaching, is through our silent life. We live for an Ideal; we believe in something which saturates our thought and absorbs all our interest, something which permeates our whole being; and it is bound to reach others. Each life is a radiating power, which has either a good or an evil influence. We are continually giving something, consciously or unconsciously. If nothing else, we give our atmosphere, which we create through our attitude of mind. Whatever we touch on the outside is influenced by our inner life. A little study will prove to us how true and tangible this influence is. According to that also do we draw evil or good things to us. These facts, however, should not discourage us in any way. On the contrary they should inspire us with new hope, because they show us that we have the power to create. We can make and unmake—we can make better conditions by our thoughts and feelings, if we are ardent and sincere; also the conditions which exist we can unmake by changing our habits of mind and body. If our misery is the product of wrong thinking or mistaken actions, then certainly we can remove it by altering the order of things and living with discrimination, thoughtfulness and nobility of purpose.

It is not a matter of studying books or subscribing to a creed or believing in a dogma. It lies far deeper. It has to do with something which abides in the human heart. Outside things have little to do with it. It deals directly with our own life. God can never become a reality for us merely because some one has said so. Only when we begin to have that feeling vividly within, in our own soul, does His reality become an established fact for us. Then no one can make us doubt. We see this in the lives of the great ones. They live for their Ideal and they die for their Ideal; but even when they die for their Ideal, death does not end their mission. In dying, they live more truly for it; because the things which are of spirit can never be annihilated.

This is something, however, which we cannot grasp theoretically. So long as we believe in material conditions and our heart craves for things pertaining to this world, we may quote from the Scriptures and talk of holy things, but our words will produce very little effect. A man may preach eloquently, advising people to renounce all evil and selfishness; but if he has within himself the least selfish instinct, he will undo his own words. Living is the watchword, it is the keynote of all spiritual philosophy and religion. Men may fight over doctrine or dogma; but when we get down to the fundamental facts of life, we find no room for discussion. As soon as we have the living consciousness of the great realities of life, then all differences vanish for us. It is only when we have not reached the depths that we dispute and condemn.

A noble character has a universal influence wherever he is born—in the East or in the West. His unselfishness, his spiritual fragrance are not limited by any boundary line. They reach all hearts which are yearning for the same qualities. The only way we surmount our own limitations and all the conditions we call evil in this world is through the living of a life which is part of Truth or God, what-

ever the name we give Him. There is but
one stupendous cosmic Fact and we are
all parts of that great Fact. When we
realize this, we realize the ideal of Father-
hood; and having realized that, we also
realize what is meant by brotherhood.
When we know that we are all children of
one divine Being, naturally we become
united. But this does not come through
mere adherance to a church or a creed;
we realize it first individually in our own
heart, and afterwards we realize it in the
universe. If, however, we do not realize
it in our own heart through devotion, we
may seek it everywhere in the world, but
we shall find it nowhere. That is why the
Indo-Aryans lay so much stress on going
within and realizing our deeper nature,
if we would attain true love for God, and
for our fellow-men.

It is good for us to get away from ourselves, to forget the physical self with its

name and form and littleness; and the
best way to do this is by seeking a spiritual Ideal. No one can dictate to you
what this Ideal should be. No one has
the right to tell you that this is the only
Ideal and you must follow it. God is
infinite and all-abiding. He is just as
much yours as any one's. He is within
you as truly as He can be anywhere.
You have just as much right to know
Him as any saint or seer ever had, but
you must awaken within you the sense
of His presence. We all have it in some
degree, just as we all have an immortal
soul; but an ignorant person does not
know it, so he constantly suffers pain
and torment. Therefore we must try to
develop our spiritual consciousness.
Whatever may be our Ideal or the form
of our faith, if we have a really yearning
desire to know the Truth, He who per-
ceives all our thoughts and innermost

feelings will surely reveal It to us. Then will such true devotion and consecration fill our hearts that we shall live, move and have our being wholly for His service, and the service of all His children.

IV.

THE PRACTICE OF SILENCE

Loud speech, profusion of words, and possessing skillfulness in expounding Scriptures are merely for the enjoyment of the learned. They do not lead to liberation.—*Sankaracharya*.

That which we most require for our spiritual growth is the silence of the desire and of the tongue before God, Who is so high: the language He most listens to is that of silent love.—*St. John of the Cross*.

Silence is as deep as eternity, speech as shallow as time.—*Carlyle*.

THE best shrine man can ever create for the Supreme is in his own heart. There are places where holiness pervades, but that which makes them holy is the human soul living in the consciousness of God. We can all create such shrines, by the absence of anger, by the practice of humility, compassion, forgiveness and faith. When every act is made an act of devotion, then quickly the living Presence is felt within. But we cannot feel this Presence except in the silence. That silence, however, is not so much external silence as the silence of our inner being.

So long as there is any unrest within us, we cannot hope to perceive or reflect the Spirit of God. Nor can we penetrate into the innermost recesses of our being. When, however, all turbulence ceases, then we grow conscious of the divine Presence and have a realization of the inner life.

There are two ways to practise silence. One is through absence of thought. The other through fullness of thought. The second is productive of great strength. When we try to empty the mind, there is danger of its falling into a dull negative state, which opens it to many possible weakening influences. This is often the origin of mental depression, melancholia and those forms of insanity which are due to obsession. When on the contrary we are able to fill the mind with one dynamic thought, not only does it fortify us against outer and inner dangers, but of itself it will empty the mind of all alien thoughts. Even a weak person by following this method will soon develop a certain tranquility and strength. There are two opposite elements constantly playing on the human mind. The one, known in Sanskrit as *Tamas,* creates a state of heaviness, dullness, indiscrimination and dejection. The other, called *Rajas,* carries the thought to the opposite extreme of over-activity, turbulence, noisy aggression and ostentation. At the point where these contending elements attain perfect balance, a third state known as *Sattwa* is produced. In this state only is true silence possible. In *Sattwa* we have the positive silence; in *Tamas,* the negative. The two kinds may seem to resemble each other outwardly. One overpowered by dullness may appear tranquil; but it is a very different condition from the serene stillness of *Sattwa,* where all the faculties of the mind are wide awake and full of light.

This higher form of silence, however, cannot be acquired in a moment. To cultivate it, we must master all our forces; and this means steady practice. First we must try so far as we can to have a healthy body, for any physical disturbance easily destroys the silence of the mind. But a healthy body is not all; a healthy mind is better; and when we have spiritual health, that is best of all. It being a less tangible form of health, people do not attach so much importance to it; yet without it, we can never have true health of mind or body.

Spiritual attainment requires great patience. It appears at times almost beyond our reach, because it seems to call for so much sacrifice; but we must make sacrifices for everything we earn on any plane; and in reality spiritual sacrifice is not so great because the return is so much richer and more enduring. Whenever we follow our higher instincts, instead of our lower, we humanize the animal in us and the noisier, more excitable part of our nature is quieted. The idea of silence is not merely avoiding action; it is bringing all our scattered and undisciplined forces wholly under our control. So long as our heart is agitated, our mind stormy and our nerves distracted, it is not possible for us to have unobstructed vision or the power of clear decision. But when the moments of stillness come, we have flashes of understanding which make our path clear.

It is interesting to note how the practice of silence enters into the heart of every vital religion. Whether it takes the form of quiet reflection, inaudible prayer or some other special ritual of worship, it has always one aim in view and that is to make the heart of the worshipper detached from the influence of the loud and distracting material world. The Quaker mystics fully realized the value of silence and carefully incorporated it in their mode of worship. The following gives an example of their faith: "First began the stilling of mind and soul. The very activity of the brain may make a man a bad listener, and listening was our goal. The intellect needs to learn how to be still, no less than the body, if it is to concentrate all its powers. This bringing of the mind away from its distractions and restlessness to a single and sustained attention on God, is the crux of the whole matter. The recollection of God under some aspect of His boundless immensity—His greatness, His awful sanctity, His en-

folding Being, His Presence in the soul
of man,—these are cosmic thoughts in
themselves casting upon the mind the
hush and still wonder which is the ave-
nue to contemplation.

"Thus we pass to the centre of our
silence. The will is at its highest activity. Just as an insect poised in the air,
seeming motionless, with wings in such
rapid motion that they are invisible, is
all the while sustained by its resistance
to the air, so the will in this listening is
not passive. It holds fast to its rest in
God by sustained resistance to all that
would drag it down or invade its silence.
This is very far from making the mind
a blank. It is the filling of the mind with
God to the exclusion of all else. Not in
words, or visions, or signs, did we
look for the communications of God.
Thoughts rising spontaneously, move-
ments and stirrings welling up from the

depths of the soul, the inner glory of God hidden in the soul of man, emerging, filling the Temple,—none of these word images conveys what can be conveyed. Only we knew God, and we knew that we knew Him."

The practice of silence has to do with every part of our system. There is a silence of the body, a silence of the mind and a silence of the heart. Until all these are tranquilized, we cannot know what true silence is. The body is silent when it is free from both motion and tension. It must be wholly relaxed, yet firm and quiet. This is gained by the practice of posture, which is one of the most essential exercises in developing the power of meditation. Posture teaches us not only to hold the body still in some fixed position at special times, but at all times to avoid every superfluous motion and maintain equilibrium. Nothing helps more to conserve our physical energies than this form of silence. It also has great healing power. The mind acquires silence through the persistent practice of discriminative elimination and concentration. As it comes in contact with the external world, it learns to distinguish between vital and non-vital, real and unreal; then discarding the unreal and non-vital, it focuses itself with ardor upon the object of its attention. The heart grows still and full of gladness through meditation, which is an unbroken flow of the thought and feeling towards the Ideal. In the inner realm serenity, not inactivity, brings the sense of silence. Perfect balance and calmness never fail to generate great power throughout the whole organism. Only in this state do we see the manifestation of the highest intelligence.

Exercises in silence are like exercises

given to soldiers; a sort of spiritual drill. Their effect must be seen in all that we do; because whatever we undertake with the aid of a well-disciplined mind, trained to absolute attention, cannot fail to be more efficiently done. This is why it is so needful for us to gain more and more the habit of silence and one-pointedness. Only so can we create an island for ourselves. The sages declare that each one can make for himself an inner island, which no storm can overwhelm. This is the purpose of all spiritual practice. Thus, if a person who is distracted with thoughts of sickness, sorrow, perplexity, can sit quietly and hold thoughts of purity and divine wisdom, very soon he will begin to feel the unbounded nature of his own soul and of the cosmic life of which he is a part; and his whole being will be filled with strength and tranquility. When we are disturbed by our association or environment, if we are able to practise silence, that is, detach our thought wholly from the distracting condition and hold it firmly on some higher thought even for a few moments, it will restore our equilibrium, we shall be lifted out of the condition and feel as if we had been bathed in fresh clear water. Whenever we spend even a moment in silent communion with our spiritual Ideal, we are revived and ready to start on our way once more.

How can we hope to hear the subtle voice of the Spirit as long as we are listening to all the noises of the world? It is not possible. That is why silence is so necessary. We must close all our senses, because it is through these doors that the sounds of the world reach us. If we wish to commune with God, we must disconnect ourselves from all distracting influences. No one is nearer to us than God, but we must know it. The more we are engrossed in the world, the less do we have the opportunity to seek Him. When we are not awake and attentive on the higher plane, things of the Spirit do not touch us. Purity of heart, openness of mind, willingness to follow: these constitute the whole of the spiritual life. When we have these, God bestows on us all His choicest gifts. We must work with one-pointed devotion, with a sense of consecration, and with unpressed heart. We must also cultivate the power to receive. Then nothing can hold us back. If we will but live a silent, prayerful life, striving to strengthen our purpose and to quiet the noisy voice of the ego within us, God will make our steps steady and unfaltering, infill us with His divine wisdom, and bless us with the consciousness of His Holy Presence.

V.

THE LIGHT WITHIN

Thou that wouldst find the Lost One, lose thyself
For naught but self divides thyself from Him,
Ask ye how I o'erpassed the dreary void?
One little step beyond myself was all.
—*Akhlaq-i-Jalali.*

All eyes can see when light flows out from God.
—*George Eliot.*

Give me the splendid silent sun, with all his beams
full dazzling.—*Whitman.*

THE object of spiritual devotion is to keep the lamp of our inner life burning brightly. Just as an ordinary lamp requires constant refilling that it may not go out, so we must feed the flame of our spiritual life by the faithful practice of devotion. If we have not the habit of such practice, the light is quickly extinguished. For this reason we are asked to have fixed hours for devotional practice; because habitual practice alone will keep it burning. It is present in every soul, but in some it is more apparent than in others. In the truly great ones it burns with steady glowing flame. It is indeed this light of the soul shining through them which makes them great.

There come moments, however, in every life when the inner spiritual lamp seems almost extinguished. We feel doubting, helpless. At such times the only way we can revive and sustain it is by conscious communion with its Source. Actually this light has no limit except that which we put upon it by our own thoughts and actions. When we remove these self-created limitations, we find that at once it gains in power and we no longer feel ourselves in darkness. We must strive, therefore, to make God a reality and learn to sustain this light within that it may never grow dim.

First we must trust in the Divine. We must believe God to be more potent

than material things and we must be
willing to give ourselves to Him. But
we cannot do this in a half-hearted way.
We must give ourselves wholly; and
when we do this, our trust grows. It is
our scatteredness and complexity which
make spiritual things appear so unat-
tainable. To the simple heart they seem
near and easy of access. Perfect trust,
however, cannot rest on hearsay. What
others tell us of God can never give us
unshakable faith. We must prove Him
for ourselves. But before we reach that
point, we need perseverance and patience; for we shall have to cross over
many obstacles. If we show any faint-
heartedness or weakness, we cannot attain the highest. When, however, we are
determined to go on with our spiritual
life and resolutely trust in God for
guidance, He sees our effort and comes
to our aid.

It does not matter how many times we fail, we must still push on. Some people become frightened at once and are thrown off their path because they meet with a little opposition. But in reality opposition is a great blessing, because it fortifies our character. If we cannot stand a little jar, how can we strengthen our will? That man is a strong man who can go through all the calamities of life unmoved. Any one can be carried away by a little joy or a little sorrow, but he who meets all things with perfect calmness has a finer element in his heart. When we learn to base the whole structure of our life on the rock of Truth, it does not matter what our conditions are; but it does matter very much that we remain loyal and ever-devoted to the great cosmic Spirit. If we do not, we are cut off from the Source. When on the contrary, we are firm in our devotion and pass through every test unshaken, then the light will shine brightly in us.

God is never partial. His mercy and grace are constantly upon us, but we do not know how to retain them. They fall away, like the rain-water that flows off a steep hillside. Only the lowly, trusting heart is able to retain the grace of God. Whenever we grow disturbed and begin to feel the injustice and misery of the world, we must always look within for the cause. When there is joy there, all the world will seem full of joy. The only salvation to be found is in our own inner being. There alone shall we find the light, as we live close to the heart of God.

One of the signs of spiritual growth is independence of external things. He who has true spiritual gifts maintains his independence no matter with what he is surrounded. The tendency of the worldly mind is to look first to material comforts; while the wise men make it their first effort to establish themselves in spiritual things. They never make the sacrifice of spirit to matter. We betray our habit of life and our attitude of mind by this,—whether we give the greatest importance in our daily living to matter or to spirit.

Whole-hearted desire forms the basis of all devotion. We must have single-hearted longing for our Ideal or we cannot be devoted. Yet what is now only on the surface can be increased and strengthened. At present with the majority of us the spiritual plane seems vague, because we have not made the effort to acquaint ourselves with it; but when we lay hold of the spiritual faculty within us and begin to cultivate that, then the things of the spirit become real to us.

Spiritual powers are as subject to culture as intellectual or physical powers. They can be developed so as to take a vital place in our life. It depends upon our mental attitude. Make God a reality and the whole life becomes consecrated. When we live in touch with the Supreme Cosmic Being, our power is renewed every hour.

Let us then lift our hearts beyond these limited conceptions of life, that they may breathe freely in the infinite expanse of God. Let us dedicate our thoughts and all our conscious and unconscious activities to Him; for when they are dedicated to the Highest, they transcend all limitations. Let us try to make our heart and mind receptive, and silence this constant play of ego which creates so much unrest in us. Let us surrender all our powers to the great Power which abides within us and which should rule us at every moment of our existence. If we can do this, then we may be sure that that light which is a part of the great Light will shine in us and drive away all darkness.

Our spiritual pursuits, when looked upon from the worldly point of view, often appear indefinite and lacking in direct evidence and we begin to doubt. But this attitude will make it more difficult to get any clear perception of Truth; for whatever we undertake with sceptical attitude will not carry us far. It is like rowing a boat without pulling up the anchor. Before we begin our higher quest, we must make the channel perfectly clear. Frequently we work on one side and leave another side unprotected. The story is told of a man who labored the whole day to water his orchard; but when the evening came, he discovered that all the water he had pumped

out had run off into two big holes and
his orchard was as dry as before. So,
often, while we think we are laboring for
spiritual things, at some point the channel is blocked and we fail to derive the
benefit we expect. If we have any hard
or hateful thoughts towards any one, no
matter how many prayers we may say
before our altar, it is impossible for any
blessing to flow to us.

Our spiritual devotion must come from
the whole heart. It is not enough to give
our prayers to God, we must also give
our thoughts and actions. Our entire
study is for this—to quicken us, so that
we may handle all our forces consciously
and direct them into higher channels.
We cannot possibly stop thinking or act-
ing; we shall continue to think and act
and perform our duties, but we shall do
it with a different point of view. All our
activities and thoughts will be conse-

crated and actuated by the higher Power which abides within us.

We must take the same thought for our spiritual welfare as we do now for our material welfare. The concern we feel at present as to what we shall have for our body to-morrow or the day after, the same concern we must feel as to what we shall have for our soul. We must cultivate a genuine fervor, an intense yearning for spiritual things. When our devotion is truly sincere, it will generate a great power; and through this we shall lift ourselves and unite ourselves with God. We must, however, first root out from the mind the false conception which makes us believe that our bodily life is the greater reality and that our material needs are of foremost importance. These ideas will fall away when we come to know the bigger facts of nature; and when we come to know the biggest fact of all, we cannot help but drop all littleness and selfishness. Then a sense of true spiritual consecration will rise spontaneously from the innermost recesses of our being.

At every hour we must strive consciously and unconsciously. You may say, how can we strive unconsciously? If we strive earnestly through our conscious hours, then in the unconscious hours our heart and mind will refuse to do anything unworthy. Thus at last our whole being will become attuned to the Supreme. We shall realize that we have come here, not to work out our own selfish ends, but to fulfil the will of God. Then all the baser instincts of our nature will be destroyed and the light within will shine in its full glory.

O Thou who art the Soul of our souls, the Light of all lights, the Ever-living and Unchanging One!

Our words of supplication, our prayers
  and thoughts go to Thee.
Manifest Thy immeasurable Glory to us.
In all humility and surrender we offer
  unto Thee our devotion.
Kindle within us a greater yearning to
  dedicate ourselves to the Highest.
We pray Thee to give us ever greater
  strength and wisdom.
Fill our hearts with compassion and the
  spirit of peace.
May peace abide in us and all love;
For by the bonds of love are we united
  with all Thy children,
And with Thee who art the storehouse of
  Infinite Love.

VI.

THE ETERNAL PRESENCE

Silence is the heart of all things; sound the fluttering
    of its pulse,
Which the fever and the spasm of the universe convulse.
Every sound that breaks the silence only makes it more
    profound,
Like a crash of deafening thunder in the sweet, blue
    stillness drowned;
Let thy soul walk softly in thee, as a saint in heaven
    unshod,
For to be alone with silence, is to be alone with God.
                —*Beyond the Sunrise.*

OUTER conditions and circumstances have very little influence upon us when we have the grasp of eternal things. When the Eternal Presence becomes a reality to us, we find our strength and inspiration even in the midst of the greatest sorrow. Not only can we meet all difficulties with calmness but we have even a sense of joyousness as we face them. Instead of being thwarted by them, we come to regard them as blessings. The power of the Spirit always rules over matter. If through the meditative life we gain higher understanding and learn to manifest our spiritual nature, material things will affect us very little. All the small undesirable elements which now disturb us will vanish and this world will become heavenly.

Who makes the world heavenly? Human beings. Through their conduct and superior understanding they can change the whole atmosphere of the world. If, instead of seeing only the material and changeable, we begin to feel more related to the eternal and unchanging, we shall awaken to a new sphere of consciousness. Yet although it may seem new, it was always there, for it is eternally existent. In the hour of loneliness or perplexity, if we can be conscious of that great Presence, we shall never feel lost. Those who cultivate such habits are never disconnected from the Source, and they become invincible. Evil does not overcome them, they overcome evil.

When we reach this state, we possess such superior strength that even the most aggressive person feels powerless before us. We cannot convince a man or turn him from his weakness merely by arguing with him or fighting him, but often we completely transform him by showing him something higher. We see this in the lives of truly great men. They are full of love and brotherly sympathy and compassion, and, above all, of the spirit of the Infinite; the small things naturally have no importance for them, so they are able to meet their fellow-men on a higher plane and they call out what is noblest in them.

When we evolve this consciousness, not only do we deal a death-blow to our own unhappiness, but also we remove a part of the world's unhappiness, because we strike another note. To be able to do this, however, we must go deep into our own nature. It is not a matter of talking and theorizing; it is a matter of finding. And where? Where can we gain access to Divinity except in our own soul? How can we make acquaintance with our inner powers except within ourselves? And this is done most effectively when our whole nature becomes silent and one-pointed. As soon as this new vista opens before us, we begin to be imbued with a new understanding. A more expanded consciousness dawns in our heart, and it is through this that we are freed from all petty feelings and iimitations. All the ethical lessons we learn through books or Scriptures, about love and charity and service, never seem to us really true and never become an inherent part of our daily life until we gain this larger consciousness. But when we have gained it, we do not fear death even; because we overcome death through a new consciousness of life, a life which is undying. We have no more fear of anything, because we have found that One Who stands supreme and that One is our own.

This consciousness of the Presence of Divinity or God is not a matter of name and form. It makes no difference by what name we call Him. It is an inner awakening, a spiritual conception. When we attain it, we drop all dispute regarding the nature of God or the nature of the soul. We believe in God because we know Him. We call Him all-loving, because we have proved His all-loving nature in our own soul. We speak of Him as almighty and infinite, because we have found Him to be so. Only when our spiritual Ideal has thus become a reality, do we become religious. We do not become religious merely by belonging to a creed or church, however lofty or noble. It is by finding this Reality within us. We can never convince any one else regarding our spiritual faith until we have convinced ourselves, and when we are absolutely convinced, we shall not need to go about preaching our faith; we shall do our preaching by our silent actions. Our conduct, our life, our every thought, our very presence will preach. Example teaches much more than words. The greatest lessons we learn about self-control are not from books, but from some one who has subdued his passions and lower propensities and shows complete mastery of himself. That living example makes an impression and we carry that impression with us.

It is a matter of living and to live Truth we must find it directly for ourselves. That is the purpose of our spiritual study and practice. Devotion, prayer, meditation, philosophic discrimination, all help us towards our spiritual upliftment that we may have direct perception of our Ideal. If we do not accomplish that, all our efforts are vain. That is, if we lose sight of the fundamental fact that realization must be our aim and goal, we may go on adding one superficial effort to another, but they will bring very small results. The spirit of Reality must be kept alive in us. We must hold fast to the sense of the Eternal Presence. But no one can do this for us. We must do it for ourselves. Let us try in all earnestness. We owe it to ourselves, for the soul's welfare should be the foremost consideration of every mortal. If we fail in this, we are failing in the fundamental principle of life, as well as in the first duty towards ourselves and towards our fellowmen.

Let us strive anew to consecrate all our thoughts and feelings to Him. He is the Eternal among all fleeting things. He is the consciousness in all conscious beings. He is the One in the midst of many. He it is Who fulfils the desires of every heart. He is the Source and Sustainer of all, the Giver of all good, the Bestower of all blessedness. May He grant us steadfast devotion and kindle in our soul the consciousness of His loving Presence, that we may never forget Him or fail to abide by His Will. May He remove from our hearts all harshness, all egotism, all discordant and alien feelings, that we may live in Him in harmony, love and peace. May His Peace be upon us and upon all living beings.